CHICAGO'S BRIDGES

Nathan Holth

SHIRE PUBLICATIONS

Published in Great Britain in 2012 by Shire Publications
Ltd, Midland House, West Way, Botley, Oxford OX2 0PH,
United Kingdom.

44-02 23rd Street, Suite 219, Long Island City, NY 11101,
USA.

E-mail: shire@shirebooks.co.uk   www.shirebooks.co.uk

A CIP catalogue record for this book is available from the
British Library.

Shire Library no. 673.   ISBN-13: 978 0 74781 103 9

Nathan Holth has asserted his right under the Copyright,
Designs and Patents Act, 1988, to be identified as the
author of this book.

Designed by Tony Truscott Designs, Sussex, UK
and typeset in Perpetua and Gill Sans.

Printed in China through Worldprint Ltd.

12 13 14 15 16   10 9 8 7 6 5 4 3 2 1

COVER IMAGE
The triangular patterns that characterize truss bridges are
clearly visible in the lowered St. Charles Air Line Railroad
Bridge and the raised Baltimore and Ohio Chicago
Terminal Railroad Bridge, both crossing the South Branch
of the Chicago River.

TITLE PAGE IMAGE
The south leaf of the Wells Street Bridge crossing the Main
Stem of the Chicago River is seen in the raised position
from Wacker Drive.

CONTENTS PAGE IMAGE
Looking east down the Main Stem of the Chicago River, at
the ornate bridge tender houses and graceful trusses of the
Clark Street Bridge.

ACKNOWLEDGEMENTS
I am grateful to the following individuals for their
assistance in reviewing the original manuscript: Frank J.
Hatfield, Nan Jackson, Vern J. Mesler, James S. Phillips,
and Susan B. Holth.

I also wish to thank Tom Winkle for volunteering himself
and his boat, allowing me to better access and photograph
a number of bridges.

The efforts of both Google and the Internet Archive to
scan and digitize old, out-of-copyright publications and
make them freely searchable and viewable online were of
great assistance in researching bridges and locating
historical photos.

Credit is due for the sketch on page 41 (bottom), adapted
from Library of Congress, Prints & Photographs Division,
HAER IL-157 (original sketch by Justin M. Spivey), as well
as the photo on page 12, from Library of Congress, Prints
& Photographs Division, HAER ILL, 16-CHIG, 133-13.

Shire Publications is supporting the Woodland Trust, the UK's leading woodland conservation charity, by funding the dedication of trees.

CONTENTS

BRIDGES THAT MOVE

STAND JUST SOUTH OF THE Michigan Avenue Bridge on a hot summer day and look north toward the "Magnificent Mile" (Chicago's Michigan Avenue) and watch countless cars, buses, and pedestrians stream across the bridge, while tour boats and water taxis packed with people pass under it. With all the activity, it may be easy not to notice that the Michigan Avenue Bridge, like dozens of bridges in Chicago, is something special. It is one of Chicago's movable bridges.

With movable bridges spanning the Calumet River and Chicago River systems in the city, it is often claimed that no other city in the world has more movable bridges than Chicago. As of 2012, well over sixty movable bridges remained in Chicago, although about half of them were no longer routinely opened for boats. Chicago was a leader in the development of movable bridges. New and improved designs originated in Chicago, and a number of Chicago's bridges set records for size or weight when completed. Engineers in Chicago designed bridges built all over the world.

The majority of bridges in the world are fixed. Fixed bridges remain in the same position at all times, and as such, fixed bridges crossing navigable waters must provide enough clearance for boats moving underneath them. In contrast, movable bridges can open to allow tall boats to pass under the bridges. Movable bridges avoid the long ramps required for a fixed bridge that is tall enough for all boats.

FIXED BRIDGES

A brief discussion of fixed bridges helps set the stage for understanding movable bridges. In the simplest sense, a bridge is composed of a superstructure, a

substructure, and a deck. The superstructure is the part of the bridge that does the actual job of spanning a feature, such as a river, road, or ravine. The substructure is the part of the bridge that holds the superstructure. Abutments are the substructure at each end of a bridge. Piers are any additional substructure supports located between the abutments. The deck is the surface upon which traffic travels.

The Ashland Avenue Bridge over the North Branch of the Chicago River displays its graceful pony truss superstructure.

Chicago's movable bridges have either a truss or a girder superstructure. Truss bridges are bridges whose superstructure is composed of triangular frameworks. Each framework is known as a truss line, which is positioned parallel to the roadway. Top chords and bottom chords run more or less horizontally at the extreme top and bottom of the truss. Between the chords are vertical and diagonal members. The exact arrangement of these members varies because engineers have devised a number of ways to configure them to make an efficient use of materials. Floor beams run between the truss lines under the roadway to hold the deck. Engineers categorize truss bridges based on the location of the truss lines in relation to the deck of a bridge.

Bridges with truss lines completely below the bridge deck are deck trusses. Bridges with truss lines above the bridge deck are pony trusses. Some bridges have trusses that are above the deck like a pony truss, but are so tall that they need special overhead bracing beams that run between the

Railing-height truss bridges such as the Wabash Avenue Bridge combine the concepts of a deck and pony truss bridge. Note how the truss extends slightly above the deck creating a guardrail between the sidewalks and roadway.

truss lines to keep them stabilized. These bridges are called through trusses. In Chicago, some trusses combine the features of a deck and pony truss by extending both below and above the deck. The portion that extends above the deck serves a dual function as a guardrail, giving rise to the railing-height truss.

In the most basic sense, girder bridges are similar to truss bridges, except that in place of a triangular framework, there is a large, solid beam called a girder. Bridges with girders located below the deck are deck girders, and bridges with girders located above the deck are through girders. A modern variation of the girder bridge has special girders that are not solid beams. Instead, four plates welded together form a hollow beam called a box girder.

MOVABLE BRIDGE TYPES

The three most common movable bridge types are the swing, vertical lift, and bascule. Although most of Chicago's movable bridges are bascule bridges, the city is home to all three types. A variety of materials can be used to build movable bridges, including wood, concrete, iron, and steel. The most commonly found materials in Chicago's movable bridges are concrete for substructure and steel for superstructure.

Swing bridges rotate horizontally on a pier that is usually located at the center of both the bridge structure and the river it crosses. Swing bridges were popular in the United States in the 1800s, with the first Chicago example appearing on Clark Street in 1854. Chicago welcomed swing bridges as replacements for troublesome floating pontoon bridges that took up space, were vulnerable to floods, and opened slowly. Although the design

and operation of swing bridges was relatively simple, the major downside of swing bridges proved to be especially problematic for Chicago. Not only did most swing bridges sit on a pier that divided the river into two narrow channels, but the width of the swing bridge itself further constricted the navigation channel, a problem that grew worse as increased highway traffic demanded wider bridges. The U.S. War Department had the power to condemn bridges on Chicago's navigable waters, and it pushed hard for the replacement of swing bridges from 1892 and into the first decades of the twentieth century, quickly making them a thing of Chicago's past.

Vertical lift bridges are those whose main structure remains level while rising to provide clearance for boats. The most common forms, including all examples in Chicago, have towers at both ends and a system of counterweights, cables, and motors that lift the bridge superstructure. The famous bridge engineer John Alexander Low Waddell and his business partner John Lyle Harrington (operating the firm Waddell and Harrington in Kansas City, Missouri) were both major promoters of this bridge type and held patents relating to them. Vertical lift bridges offered an improvement

Built in 1900 and 334.5 feet long, the railroad bridge crossing the Chicago Sanitary and Ship Canal east of Cicero Avenue is one of a small number of surviving swing bridges in Chicago.

Appearing in a photo published in 1892, this through truss swing bridge carried State Street over the Main Stem of the Chicago River until replaced by a bascule bridge. Chicago once had many similar swing bridges.

7

This portrait of bridge engineer and vertical lift bridge advocate John Alexander Low Waddell appeared in his well-known publication *Bridge Engineering* in 1916.

over swing bridges, providing a navigation channel unobstructed by a center pier. Because the bridge remains directly over the waterway even when raised for boats, the bridge must be designed to rise high enough to provide adequate vertical clearance. Vertical lift bridges were a relatively costly investment, and from the late nineteenth century through the twentieth century, they found only occasional use in Chicago as an alternative to the vastly more popular bascule bridge.

Bascule is a French word for "seesaw." Movable bridges that rotate upward to provide an opening for boats are called bascule bridges because they operate somewhat like a seesaw, using a counterweight at one end to provide balance. A bascule bridge may have one "leaf," which rises up, or two leaves, the latter being called a double-leaf bascule. Bascule bridge designs vary in construction and operation and are categorized accordingly, often named after the engineer who invented a particular design. In Chicago, the three most common types are the fixed trunnion, the Strauss heel-trunnion, and the Scherzer rolling lift.

Despite greater cost and engineering effort, railroads preferred the rigidity of single-leaf bascule bridges to carry heavy trains. Double-leaf bascule bridges were stable enough for highway traffic, and the city believed they were more aesthetically pleasing. Nearly all the highway bascule bridges in Chicago are double-leaf, while all of Chicago's railroad bascule bridges are single-leaf.

A sailboat passes under a raised Dearborn Street Bridge, a double-leaf bascule with railing-height trusses.

COMPETING BASCULE BRIDGES AND THEIR BUILDERS

A TRUNNION BASCULE BRIDGE is a bridge that has a leaf or leaves that lift by rotating around a giant axle called a trunnion. On one side of the trunnion is the main span of the bridge, and on the other side is the counterweight, which balances the weight of the leaf over the trunnion. With a fixed trunnion bascule, the counterweight is rigidly connected to the bascule leaf, and there is a single trunnion, which is the pivot around which the leaf rotates. The trunnion itself does not move. Chicago's fixed trunnion bascule bridges are designed so that the counterweights are always hidden under the roadway in a tail pit. A rack and pinion system, usually driven by electric motors, puts the bridge into motion.

Chicago designed its own fixed trunnion bascule bridges, rather than hiring one of the many consulting engineers and bridge companies operating in the twentieth century. The city made the effort to design its own type of bascule as it sought ways to provide a reliable, wide channel for navigation along its rivers and canals and to avoid the cost of an outside firm and a patented design. Other cities and highway agencies soon copied Chicago's general design of fixed trunnion bascule, and this bascule subtype became commonly known as the Chicago trunnion type of bascule. Nearly all movable highway bridges in Chicago are fixed trunnion bascule bridges. In this book, it is assumed that a highway bascule bridge in Chicago is of the fixed trunnion type unless otherwise specified.

Except for four years, John Ernst Ericson was Chicago's city engineer from 1897 to 1927.

Of the many people who contributed to the development of Chicago's trunnion bascule bridges, three people stand out as the most noteworthy. John Ernst Ericson was born in Sweden on October 21, 1858, and immigrated to the United States in 1881. After holding a variety of jobs and positions, he became Chicago's city engineer in 1897. Thomas G. Pihlfeldt was born in Norway on October 11, 1858, and moved to Chicago in 1879. He began to work for the city in 1889, and in 1901, became Chicago's engineer of bridges. In this position, he played a major

Thomas Pihlfeldt became Chicago's engineer of bridges in 1901. He played a major role in the design of Chicago's movable highway bridges until his death in 1941.

role in the design of Chicago's bridges. Alexander F. L. von Babo was born on May 27, 1854, in Germany and immigrated to the United States in 1886. By 1900, he was working for Chicago as an engineer of bridge design.

In 1899, Ericson directed his department to find a better movable bridge design for the city. With the assistance of a hired board of consulting engineers, they decided on the fixed trunnion bascule bridge. The famous Tower Bridge in London is an earlier example of a fixed trunnion bascule, albeit one that utilizes a very costly design. Chicago's engineers developed a more cost-effective fixed trunnion bascule. Although Chicago did not invent the fixed trunnion bascule, they made it economical for typical movable bridge crossings. Von Babo appears to have played a significant role in the design work that resulted in Chicago's unique variation of trunnion bascule. In 1911, he secured a patent that outlined the key characteristics of Chicago's trunnion bascule bridges.

So successful was the city in its endeavor to develop and build a new form of bascule that its bridges garnered national attention in the first couple decades of the twentieth century. Fixed trunnion bascule bridges were built in locations throughout the United States, some designed by City of Chicago engineers. Wishing to profit further from the city's innovative bascule design, Pihlfeldt and Hugh E. Young, a Chicago engineer of bridge design, began engineering consulting on the side, and in 1920 started the Chicago Bascule Bridge Company. They provided engineering services for bridges beyond the city of Chicago, including three highway bascule bridges built in the 1920s on the River Rouge in Detroit, Michigan.

The design of fixed trunnion bascule bridges built by the City of Chicago went through a series of structural and aesthetic improvements over many decades. The earliest bridges, built between 1901 and 1910, are all through trusses. The gracefully curved top chord contrasts with the seemingly random geometry of the overhead bracing. The rack and pinion for these earliest bridges is located on the outside of the truss, which limited the types of trusses the city could design. Moving the rack and pinion to the inside of the trusses allowed the city to abandon the original through truss design. As a result, in the 1910s, city engineers began designing pony trusses and later railing-height trusses, both of which found use throughout most of the remaining history of bascule bridge construction in Chicago. The earliest pony truss bridges lacked a gracefully curved top chord, but the design later matured into a more elegant form. In contrast, the design of the streamlined railing-height truss went largely unchanged through its history.

Bridges that move require workers, known as bridge tenders, to monitor movable bridges and operate the controls to raise and lower them as needed.

The buildings that house the controls to operate the bridges are called bridge tender houses. To allow bridge tenders a clear view of the river and bridge deck, bridge tender houses may be up to several stories in height, with the controls typically located at the top of the building in a windowed room. Bridge tender houses also may contain electrical and mechanical equipment to power the bridge. In Chicago, early bridge tender houses were small wooden buildings, but they became elaborate and ornate structures from 1915 and into the 1930s. After that period, they gradually became simpler and more utilitarian, adjusting to changing architectural tastes and priorities.

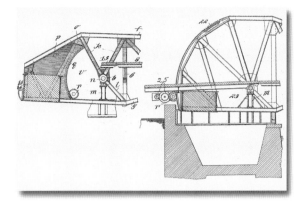

SCHERZER ROLLING LIFT BASCULE BRIDGES

Another popular type of bascule bridge is the Scherzer rolling lift. To achieve vertical rotation, a Scherzer rolling lift bascule bridge rolls backward on a track. There are no trunnions. The leaf extends outward over the crossing on one side of the track, and on the other side a counterweight is rigidly attached to the leaf to provide balance.

William Scherzer, the inventor of the rolling lift bridge, was born January 27, 1858, in Peru, Illinois, about 100 miles southwest of Chicago. He derived a broad engineering experience from four years of civil engineering education at the Polytechnicum at Zurich, Switzerland, followed by employment at several businesses including eight years at Andrew Carnegie's Keystone Bridge Company and Carnegie Steel Company. By 1893, Scherzer had left Carnegie and moved to Chicago to work as a consulting engineer. One of his last projects before his death at age thirty-five from "an attack of brain fever" was the invention of the rolling lift bascule bridge. His rolling lift bascule provided the Metropolitan West Side Elevated with a bridge to carry its railroad tracks over the South Branch of the Chicago River without interfering with the operation of swing bridges at Jackson and Van Buren streets. Scherzer also designed a similar bridge to replace the swing span at Van Buren Street. These bridges represented the initial introduction of a modern bascule bridge to Chicago.

Alexander von Babo secured a patent for Chicago's design of fixed trunnion bascule in 1911. The patent's labeled drawings show the bascule parts of the early through truss designs including racks (q, 22), pinions (r), trunnion (b), and counterweight (15).

William Scherzer (left) and his brother Albert Scherzer, as they appeared in *Men of Illinois* in 1902.

A bridge that no longer exists, the Metropolitan West Side Elevated Railroad Bridge over the South Branch of the Chicago River, is shown lowered and raised. Completed in 1895, it was the first Scherzer rolling lift bascule ever constructed.

The rolling lift bascule bridge did not die with William Scherzer. Albert Scherzer, his younger brother and president of the Scherzer Rolling Lift Bridge Company, promoted the bridge type following William's death. Albert Scherzer was born July 22, 1865, and graduated from Chicago's Union College of Law. When his brother died, Albert took on the work of running the company that William had started, while striving to make himself an expert in the movable bridge world. Despite tight competition with rival companies like the Strauss Bascule Bridge Company, the Scherzer Rolling Lift Bridge Company did well as it constructed numerous bascule bridges in locations around the world and held many patents relating to bascule bridges.

Although the impact of the Scherzer rolling lift bascule on Chicago bridges is not highly visible today, Scherzer rolling lift bascule bridges were among the first in Chicago to demonstrate that the bascule bridge was a significant improvement over the swing bridge. However, Scherzer rolling lift bascule bridges built in Chicago suffered because of abutments that deteriorated rapidly. This was caused by the relatively unstable soil conditions found in Chicago, combined with the fact that when a Scherzer rolling lift bascule bridge is raised, its center of gravity changes. Between the soil conditions and the constant shifting of weight, the abutments simply did not last.

Although a number of Scherzer rolling lift bascule bridges were built in Chicago, most have been replaced with newer trunnion bascule bridges. Fixed trunnion bascule bridges maintain the same center of gravity during operation and thus avoid the abutment problems found with Scherzer rolling lift bascule bridges.

STRAUSS HEEL-TRUNNION BASCULE BRIDGES
Joseph Baermann Strauss, born January 9, 1870, in Cincinnati, Ohio, was another competing inventor and builder of bascule bridges. In 1892, he

graduated from the University of Cincinnati with a degree in economics and business. His initial work on bascule bridges began with employment by the noted bridge engineer Ralph Modjeski. In 1902, Strauss formed the Strauss Bascule and Concrete Bridge Company. The company name reflected his interest not only in steel bascule bridges, but also in the use of concrete in bridge construction, which was relatively new at that time. He later refined his focus to bascule bridges and renamed the company Strauss Bascule Bridge Company.

Strauss's ingenuity and creativity is evident in the dozens of patents he secured, covering a wide range of topics, but with a focus on things that move. His patents included a roller coaster, a "flying machine," a special door for a prison, and numerous bascule bridge designs. The patents for movable bridges were important business tools for Strauss, allowing the Strauss Bascule Bridge Company to collect royalties and, if necessary, sue anyone who attempted to build a bascule bridge that used any of the patented features without paying royalties. In the 1910s, the City of Chicago was unfortunate enough to become involved in such a lawsuit, having employed a method for supporting the trunnions of some of its bascule bridges that was similar to a Strauss patent. Strauss successfully won a lawsuit against the city, forcing Chicago to design a new support system for its later bridges.

Joseph Strauss as he appeared in the 1910 publication *Notable Men of Chicago and Their City*.

Strauss's most significant contribution to the movable bridge world is the heel-trunnion bascule bridge, distinctly different from the fixed trunnion bascule bridge design. The Strauss heel-trunnion bascule bridges stand out by their use of a separate trunnion to support an overhead counterweight. This allows the counterweight to rotate on its own, separately from the bascule leaf as the bridge is raised or lowered. This design made a more efficient use of materials and space, made longer bascule spans possible, and decreased the cost of shorter bascule spans. The design also kept the counterweight from reaching the ground when the leaf was raised, eliminating the need for a tail pit.

This small plaque mounted on the bridge tender house of the Jackson Boulevard Bridge identifies it as a patented Strauss trunnion bascule bridge.

Strauss was more than an engineer working with equations, running calculations, and creating dimensioned drawings. In his spare time, Strauss also demonstrated an artistic ability as he composed poetry. In 1921, he produced a compilation of his poetry titled *By-Products of Idle Hours*. One of his poems, written in 1912, focuses on Chicago and suggests that Strauss was very fond of the city. The prosperous city he describes remains prosperous today, a city united by movable bridges.

STRAUSS TRUNNION BASCULE BRIDGE
PATENT NO. 995813 ISSUED JUNE 20 1911
OPERATED UNDER LICENSE
FROM
THE STRAUSS BASCULE BRIDGE CO.
CHICAGO

"Chicago"

Chicago the peerless, the wonder of earth,
Arrayed in the splendor that crowned her rebirth;
The Queen of the Inland, with realm spreading wide,
From Lakes to the Gulfland, to far mountain side;
Imperial she reigns o'er her rich dowered lands
That ceaseless their tribute pour into her hands;
Unbounded the treasure that floats to her shores,
That streams through the highways stretched out from her doors;
A kingdom of plenty, great, glorious and fair,
Her crest the rare badge only world-leaders wear;
Chicago the regal, the magical grown,
Chicago triumphant, America's own.
—Joseph B. Strauss, 1912

ARCHITECTS AND CONTRACTORS

Charles Louis Strobel as he appeared in *Men of Illinois* in 1902. His engineering and contracting firm Strobel Steel Construction Company erected the superstructures for a number of movable Chicago bridges.

The *Plan of Chicago*, a publication produced in 1909 by architects Daniel Hudson Burnham and Edward Herbert Bennett, significantly influenced the physical development of Chicago. This city planning document suggested a number of improvements to Chicago, with a focus on improving infrastructure and the artistic beauty of the city. It also was successful in convincing city leaders to establish the Chicago Plan Commission, which promoted these ideas. Although not all of the recommendations outlined in the *Plan of Chicago* were implemented, the publication itself and the Chicago Plan Commission exerted significant influence on the layout of the city. Bennett continued to work directly with the city following publication of the plan until 1930, and he had a great influence on the architectural elements of bridges built in the city. The design of many of Chicago's bascule bridges reflects Bennett's preference for the Beaux-Arts architectural style.

In addition to the engineers and architects who designed Chicago's movable bridges, it is important to recognize those who were involved with their construction. The embossed names of the mills that produced the steel are often visible on the beams of bridges. In addition to listing engineers and other officials, plaques mounted on most of the city's bridges list the contractors who erected them. Due to the complexity of movable bridges, there often were separate contractors for the superstructure, substructure, and electrical systems of a movable bridge. It was the effort of steel workers, craftsmen, and contractors that turned the drawings of engineers into reality.

NORTH BRANCH
CHICAGO RIVER TOUR

T HE CHICAGO RIVER is a 156-mile system of rivers and canals that includes the Main Stem of the Chicago River and the North and South branches of the Chicago River. The North Branch of the Chicago River extends northward from downtown Chicago. It includes the short North Branch Canal, completed in 1857 to bypass a bend in the river. Movable bridges on the North Branch of the Chicago River no longer regularly operate for boats; many are permanently fixed, their operating equipment removed.

Starting at the Deering Bridge, just west of Ashland Avenue, and moving southbound down the river, this tour begins with the first remaining movable bridge on the river. The Strauss Bascule Bridge Company designed this

The single leaf Deering Bridge is a Strauss heel-trunnion bascule. The bridge uses two concrete counterweights seen to the right.

The bas-relief sculptures on the Ashland Avenue Bridge recognize different aspects of the bascule bridge including the superstructure, bridge tender building, and mechanical equipment. This sculpture features the superstructure.

imposing railroad bridge, a Strauss heel-trunnion bascule, to replace a swing bridge. The replacement bridge is 186 feet long with a 145-foot span. Contractors constructed the Deering Bridge in the raised position, so as not to block trains on the old swing bridge, which remained open to railroad traffic during construction. So important was maintaining railroad traffic that when the bridge was completed in 1916, contractors first quickly demolished just enough of the swing bridge to lower the new bridge before continuing the demolition. Trains experienced a closure of fewer than eighteen hours as a result.

Constructed in 1936, the Ashland Avenue Bridge over the North Branch of the Chicago River with its smoothly curved pony trusses is one of the most beautiful pony truss bascule bridges in the city. The walls of the two bridge tender houses include small bas-relief sculptures that artistically depict various aspects of the bridge's function. In contrast, the 1916 Webster Avenue Bridge, located at a 90-degree angle to the nearby Ashland Avenue Bridge, is an example of the earliest style of pony truss bascule in Chicago, a less graceful design.

While its truss superstructure presents the rhythmic geometry inherent to the design, the Webster Avenue Bridge lacks the artistic embellishment of the adjacent Ashland Avenue Bridge.

Originally called the West Clybourn Place Bridge when contractors completed it by December 19, 1901, the Cortland Street Bridge is the first example of a Chicago fixed trunnion bascule ever constructed, making it a

nationally significant historic bridge. The completion of this 128-foot span marked the debut of a bridge type that would spread throughout Chicago and the entire country. It displays the through truss design typical of the earliest Chicago bascule bridges.

In 1899, Onward Bates, the Chicago, Milwaukee, and St. Paul Railway's engineer and superintendent of bridges and buildings, designed a replacement for Bridge Z-6, an aging railroad bridge south of the Cortland Street Bridge. The bridge Bates designed has a deck plate girder superstructure and is a rare example of an asymmetrical bobtail swing bridge. Rather than having a symmetrical swing bridge that rests on a center pier, a bobtail swing bridge has a superstructure that extends from the pier in one direction, while on the other side of the pier is a shorter arm that is designed as a counterweight. The crossing is located at a sharp bend in the river. It was important that there be no obstructive pier in the navigation channel, yet because of the bend in the river, building a symmetrical swing bridge with

The Cortland Street Bridge, the first Chicago fixed trunnion bascule bridge, has been rehabilitated and preserved as a historic landmark. It no longer lifts for boats but continues to carry vehicular and pedestrian traffic.

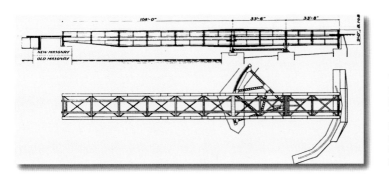

These drawings of Bridge Z-6 show its unusual design. The top-down (plan) view shows the two arcs on which the bridge rotates.

Onward Bates was born in Missouri in 1850 and was engineer and superintendent of bridges and buildings for the Chicago, Milwaukee, and St. Paul Railway from 1888 to 1901.

its pier on the shore still would have partially blocked the river when opened 90 degrees. In contrast, a bobtail swing bridge did not block the channel when opened. An unusual design feature of this bridge is that instead of resting on a single circular rim that allows for 90 degrees of rotation, the replacement Bridge Z-6 sits on two arcs that allow for only a fraction of that rotation. Due to the angle at which the railroad crosses the river, the bridge does not need to rotate a full 90 degrees to open the channel.

The North Avenue Bridge was long one of Chicago's few remaining bascule bridges that followed the city's earliest fixed trunnion bascule design. Like all of the earliest fixed trunnion bridges in the city, it had a through truss superstructure with one truss line on each side of the roadway and a third truss line in the center, and was essentially a prototype of a design that the city would embrace and perfect over future decades. The bridge had a span of 173 feet between trunnions and an overall length of 273 feet. In 2006, Chicago demolished and replaced this bridge with a fixed span.

The busy North Avenue Bridge was built in 1907 and demolished in 2006 a few months after this photo was taken.

The Cherry Avenue Bridge spans 120 feet between abutments, and the overall length of the truss including counterweight is 230 feet. The counterweight, located at the northern end of the bridge, is visible to the right.

Completed in 1902, the Cherry Avenue Bridge is a railroad swing bridge whose single deck once carried motor vehicles as well. Designed by the Chicago, Milwaukee, and St. Paul Railway, the bridge, with its through truss superstructure, is a bobtail swing bridge. The bridge has a counterweight made of concrete, an early use of concrete instead of cast iron or steel for this purpose in movable bridge construction. In 2009, the city restored, repainted, and converted this bridge into a unique, shared-use bridge that serves both nonmotorized traffic as well as the occasional train, making the bridge accessible to the public.

Chicago's municipal device is visible on the overhead bracing of the Division Street Bridge over the North Branch Canal, the only bridge with this symbol on its bracing.

Previous pages:
The Halsted Street
Bridge crossing
North Branch
Canal displays
its graceful curves
viewed from
Division Street.

Division Street crosses Goose Island (the only island on the Chicago River), which means that it must cross both the North Branch of the Chicago River on the western side of the island as well as the North Branch Canal. Both crossings are excellent and rare examples of the earliest design of Chicago fixed trunnion bascule. The 1904 river bridge is a typical example of the early bascule bridges, while the 1903 canal bridge stands out for different reasons. It has unique overhead bracing which features decorative cutout designs that display a special symbol that represents Chicago and more specifically, Wolf Point, where the three branches of the Chicago River come together. As described in the municipal code, "The municipal device, for use by the varied unofficial interests of the city and its people, shall show a Y-shaped figure in a circle, colored and designed to suit individual tastes and needs." The municipal device appears in various forms on a number of buildings and structures throughout the city, including several bridges.

Like Division Street, Halsted Street also crosses Goose Island and thus both the North Branch Canal and the North Branch of the Chicago River. As recently as 2010, this section also featured two bascule bridges. The canal bridge was built in 1909 and was an excellent example of the earliest Chicago bascule bridge design, although its bridge tender house had been removed

The concrete bridge tender house of the Chicago Avenue Bridge is visible to the right.

22

from the bridge after the city stopped raising the bridge for boats. The bridge
has an impressive span of 205.6 feet between trunnions. In 2010, the city
demolished and replaced the bridge with a fixed bridge. To the south, the
Halsted Street crossing of the river is a deck truss bascule built in 1957,
making it a late example of this design in Chicago. Red brick provides a facing
for both the bridge abutments and the single bridge tender house.

The Chicago Avenue Bridge opened to traffic in 1914 following the
completion of a $260,000 project to replace a former swing bridge that had
been condemned by the U.S. Department of War. The bridge has two bridge
tender houses, one at the northeast corner and another at the southwest
corner. The southwest building has been altered, but the northeast building
retains its original design. This bridge represents the first use of concrete for
a bridge tender house, which in turn represents a transition from simple
wooden buildings to more permanent and aesthetically pleasing building
designs. The bridge has a span of 189 feet between trunnions.

The Ohio Street Bridge is a deck truss bascule that functions as two
separate superstructures sharing the same abutments. The skew at which
Ohio Street crosses the North Branch of the Chicago River is accommodated
by offsetting the two leaves, which requires separate trunnions. The bridge

The skew of the
Ohio Street Bridge
is barely
discernable when
viewed here from
Grand Avenue.

The Kinzie Street Bridge has a strikingly asymmetrical appearance because of its single-leaf design. Wooden dolphins, like those that caused the Chicago Flood of 1992, are visible in the foreground.

dates to 1961 and has two bridge tender houses, which are simple in appearance, reflecting typical period architecture. Viaducts provide the approaches to the bridge.

Opened in 1914, the Grand Avenue Bridge is an early pony truss bascule bridge. In more recent years, the city reconstructed the bridge tender houses to restore their appearance to the original wooden design that was typical for the earliest bascule bridges in the city.

Chicago rebuilt the bridge tender house for the Grand Avenue Bridge to restore it to its original appearance. This simple building is typical of the bridge tender houses found on Chicago's earlier bascule bridges.

A rare example of Chicago's earliest style of fixed trunnion bascule, the Kinzie Street Bridge also stands out as one of only two extant single-leaf highway bascule bridges in Chicago. The bridge has a span of 136 feet from the trunnion. The Kinzie Street Bridge played a role in the infamous Chicago Flood of 1992.

In 1991, contractors were installing bundles of wooden piles, known as dolphins, around the bridge

24

to protect the abutments from boat collisions. Unknowingly, they drove the piles next to an old freight tunnel, which had been reduced to use only as an electrical utility tunnel. The piles damaged the tunnel, and by 1992, the river managed to breach the tunnel, causing a devastating underground flood throughout the tunnel system that also swamped the basements of numerous buildings in the downtown area connected to the tunnel system. Because of the electrical systems in the tunnel, officials evacuated the Loop and cut power for several days while repairing the damage and draining the tunnels.

The imposing bridge immediately south of Kinzie Street rests on the location of two bridges significant in Chicago's history: the city's first railroad bridge, which dated to 1852, and its replacement, one of the first all-steel railroad bridges in the United States, built in 1879. The Strauss Bascule and Concrete Bridge Company designed the current bascule bridge, which opened in 1908. This single-leaf bascule bridge is a prototypical example of Joseph Strauss's unique variation of trunnion bascule that evolved into the heel-trunnion design. With its 170-foot span, this bridge was also the longest and heaviest bascule leaf in the world when completed. Now it sits abandoned in the raised position.

In raised position, the through truss superstructure of the railroad bridge at Kinzie Street points to the sky, while the concrete counterweight is near the ground.

MAIN STEM
CHICAGO RIVER
TOUR

The enormous
Merchandise Mart
looms over the
Franklin Street
Bridge viewed
from Wacker
Drive.

O NLY ABOUT 1.5 miles long, the Main Stem of the Chicago River, often
called the Main Branch of the Chicago River, extends west from Lake
Michigan in downtown Chicago. This tour proceeds east from Wolf Point,
where the North, South, and Main branches of the Chicago River meet.
Bridges on the Main Stem of the Chicago River open at scheduled times in
the spring and autumn, mainly to let recreational sailboats in and out of
Lake Michigan.

The first bridge on this tour is the Franklin Street Bridge, also known as the Franklin-Orleans Bridge because it connects Franklin Street south of the river to Orleans Street north of the river. Built in 1920, this graceful pony truss bascule with a relatively long span of 252 feet has two handsome bridge tender houses and retains ornate railings for the sidewalk.

The Wells Street Bridge as seen from Franklin Street.

Similar in appearance to the Lake Street Bridge on the South Branch of the Chicago River, the 1922 double-deck Wells Street Bridge is a few years newer. The bridge is one of only two movable bridges in Chicago that carry Chicago Transit Authority (CTA) "L" (elevated) trains. The trains run on the upper deck, and vehicular and pedestrian traffic use the lower deck. Chicago Engineer of Bridges Thomas Pihlfeldt used his experience with building the Lake Street Bridge to build the Wells Street Bridge with minimal disruption of traffic. The bridge replaced an 1888 steam-powered double-deck swing bridge that carried the Northwestern Elevated Railroad on an upper deck. Today, only two other city bascule bridges, the Columbus Drive Bridge and the Wabash Avenue Bridge, surpass its trunnion-to-trunnion span of 268 feet. When built in 1922, the Wells Street Bridge was the city's heaviest bascule bridge with two truss lines. Two 100-horsepower motors that ran on 600 volts of DC current originally powered the bridge. Engineers originally designed the bridge to have a backup power source, a common practice at the time. In this case, power came from both the elevated railroad and the standard surface lines. Although the city designed the bridge, it had to secure a license from the Strauss Bascule Bridge Company to build and operate the

Overleaf:
The opening of the mighty leaves of the Wells Street Bridge is an impressive sight.

27

bridge due to similarities between the city's design and patents held by the company.

The beautiful bridges at LaSalle Street and Clark Street have the same graceful pony truss design, shared only by the Ashland Avenue Bridge over the North Branch of the Chicago River. Many of the pony truss bascule bridges in Chicago have an attractive curved design. While most have two abrupt changes in curvature at the ends of the trusses, the bridges at LaSalle and Clark streets display smoothly flowing curves at their ends.

Completed in 1931, the Clark Street Bridge has two elaborate bridge tender houses, while the 1928 LaSalle Street Bridge has four bridge tender houses that are of similar but even more ornate design. The unique mansard roof seen on the bridge tender houses of the LaSalle Street Bridge gives them a very tall appearance. In 1999, officials named the bridge at LaSalle Street the Marshall Suloway Bridge after a Chicago chief engineer and commissioner of public works.

The Dearborn Street Bridge, State Street Bridge, and Wabash Avenue Bridge all feature comparable railing-height trusses, despite different

The view looking south at the LaSalle Street Bridge with the Chicago Board of Trade Building in the far distance is among Chicago's most dramatic scenes.

construction dates. In contrast, the architectural design of their bridge tender houses and sidewalk railings varies considerably, displaying the style of the period in which each bridge was constructed. All three bridges have received awards or been honorably mentioned by the American Institute of Steel Construction for their beauty. The Dearborn Street Bridge, with its single unembellished bridge tender house and sidewalk railings, was built

in 1963, one of the last bascule bridges built in the city to use rivets and trusses. A plaque on the bridge shows and describes the first movable bridge built in Chicago, which was located at Dearborn Street and dated to 1834.

The bridge tender house for the Wabash Avenue Bridge contains the controls used to operate the bridge.

State Street Bridge, built in 1949, honors soldiers who fought in the Philippines during World War II with its official name, the Bataan-Corregidor Memorial Bridge. It features two bridge tender houses whose exteriors include depictions of the first bridge at the location, a swing bridge built in 1864, and the current bridge. With its impressive overall width of 108 feet, the State Street Bridge is wider than the Dearborn and Wabash Avenue bridges and has three truss lines.

The Wabash Avenue Bridge, constructed in 1930, features impressive Beaux-Arts bridge tender houses that were typical for that period in Chicago. The bridge today displays replicas of the original decorative pedestrian railings. In the past, the *Chicago Sun-Times* building, erected in the 1950s, stood next to the bridge, where the Trump Tower, completed in 2009, stands today. The official name of the bridge is the Irv Kupcinet Bridge, honoring a *Sun-Times* columnist. With a length of 269 feet between trunnions, it is one of the longest bascule spans in Chicago. The Dearborn Street, State Street, and Wabash Avenue bridges together make an interesting comparison to each other. It speaks to the effectiveness of the design that the city employed essentially the same truss superstructure design for more than forty years, a remarkable length of time in bridge construction.

Marina City to the left and Trump Tower to the right frame a night view of the State Street Bridge's bridge tender house.

Like many of Chicago's movable bridges, the Wabash Avenue Bridge has a plaque that provides information about the bridge's construction. The lower plaque is an award from the American Institute of Steel Construction.

Officially renamed the DuSable Bridge in 2010 to honor Jean Baptiste Pointe DuSable, Chicago's first non-native settler, the Michigan Avenue Bridge was an improvement proposed by the *Plan of Chicago* intended to transform the already popular Michigan Avenue into a primary vehicular and pedestrian corridor. Prior to the completion of the bridge in 1920, Michigan Avenue ended at the southern bank of the Chicago River. North of the river, Pine Street continued north, slightly east of where Michigan Avenue would have run if it continued straight across the river. There was no bridge at this exact location, but a short distance to the west a bridge crossed the river at Rush Street. The Michigan Avenue Bridge provided a replacement for the Rush Street Bridge and a direct connection between Pine Street and Michigan Avenue. For consistency, officials renamed Pine Street to Michigan Avenue. Because of the slight misalignment between Michigan Avenue and Pine Street, the Michigan Avenue Bridge does not cross the river exactly on the north–south axis.

Michigan Avenue intersects Wacker Drive near the bridge, where both roads are two levels. As a result of this configuration, the Michigan Avenue Bridge is a double-deck bridge that carries vehicular and pedestrian traffic on two levels. Originally, there were no sidewalks on the lower level. While the roadway layout of the bridge gives the appearance of a single structure, the actual superstructure is comprised of two parallel bascule bridges that share common abutments. As a result, it is possible to raise the northbound lanes while leaving the southbound lanes lowered and vice versa. This allows repair

The Michigan Avenue Bridge displays ornate replica railings and flags on the bridge, with the southeast bridge tender house in the distance.

or maintenance projects to raise half of the bridge while keeping the other half open to traffic. The bridge has a span of 256 feet between trunnions.

Perhaps the most visually distinctive features of the Michigan Avenue Bridge are the four bridge tender houses. These works of art each include bas-relief sculptures that recall significant events in the history of Chicago.

Regeneration, on the southeastern bridge tender house, commemorates the rebuilding of Chicago after the Great Chicago Fire of 1871. The sculpture shows several workers and craftsmen. Among them, visible toward the left side of the sculpture, is a worker using a pneumatic rivet hammer to drive a rivet into a steel beam. Rivets were used by workers to connect the parts of the majority of Chicago's movable bridges, including the Michigan Avenue Bridge. *Defense*, on the southwestern bridge tender house, is a memorial to the defenders of Fort Dearborn during the Massacre of 1812, a graphic depiction of the battle that took place during the War of 1812 with Great Britain. *The Pioneers*, on the northwestern bridge tender house, celebrates early area settlers John Kinzie and Jean Baptiste Pointe DuSable. Finally, *The Discoverers*, on the northeastern bridge tender house, commemorates explorers who passed through the Great Lakes and the Chicago area. Pictured are Louis Joliet, Jacques Marquette, René-Robert Cavelier, Sieur de La Salle, and Henri de Tonti. William Wrigley, Jr., commissioned James Earle Fraser to create the sculptures on the northern bridge tender houses. Wrigley's involvement is unsurprising given that he constructed the adjacent Wrigley Building as the headquarters for his chewing gum company around the same time that Chicago was building the bridge. The B. F. Ferguson Monument Fund commissioned Henry Hering to create the sculptures on the southern bridge tender houses. All four sculptures were installed in 1928. Bridge tenders never used the southwestern and northeastern bridge tender houses, which were built primarily for aesthetic reasons.

Today, the bridge's ornate décor and location amidst other beloved Chicago landmarks such as the Wrigley Building make the Michigan Avenue Bridge one of Chicago's most familiar. The fact that the city flies U.S., Illinois, and Chicago flags from the bridge further enhances its iconic status. In 2009, the city rehabilitated the bridge and placed new sidewalk railings on the upper level that emulate the ornamental details of the original railings, which had been replaced many years before with plain, utilitarian railings.

The northwest bridge tender house of the Michigan Avenue Bridge features *The Discoverers* and shows the ornate design typical of all four bridge tender houses.

The sculpture *Regeneration* on the Michigan Avenue Bridge includes a man riveting a steel beam like those found on many of Chicago's bridges. The riveter is the second person from the left.

The 1982 Columbus Drive Bridge, officially named William P. Fahey Bridge in honor of a police officer who in that same year lost his life in the line of duty, with its strikingly simple appearance typical of modern bridges, has a deck box girder superstructure. The single box-shaped bridge tender house has an exterior of granite panels that appear to merge into the granite panels of the abutment. The bridge won an award for its design in 1984 from the American Institute of Steel Construction.

The Lake Shore Drive Bridge is the final bridge on the river and was officially named the Franklin Delano Roosevelt Memorial Bridge in 1982 to honor the centennial anniversary of the birth of the president who dedicated the bridge. The *Plan of Chicago* outlined a plan to make Lake Shore Drive into a major connector between parks along Lake Michigan. Construction of the mighty bridge began in 1931, but due to the Great Depression, construction stopped for several years until the Works Progress Administration provided funding for the project to continue. The bridge was completed in 1937. Joseph Strauss of the Strauss Engineering Company was a consulting engineer for the project. The bridge boasts significant dimensions: a 264-foot span between trunnions, a 108-foot overall width, and leaves weighing 6,420 tons each. It set a record for heaviest bascule bridge when completed. It remains today an impressive structure with four imposing bridge tender houses surrounding the massive double-deck bridge. Due to its generous width, the bridge contains four truss lines.

The large and imposing bridge tender houses of the Lake Shore Drive Bridge almost succeed in making the trusses look less massive than they really are.

SOUTH BRANCH CHICAGO RIVER TOUR

THE SOUTH BRANCH of the Chicago River extends southward from downtown Chicago. It includes the short South Fork of the South Branch of the Chicago River, also called Bubbly Creek, a descriptive name given to it in the early twentieth century when area stockyards dumped unused animal material in the river where it decomposed, producing gas bubbles.

This tour begins at Wolf Point and works southward down the river. The Lake Street Bridge is a double-deck bascule bridge similar to the Wells Street Bridge on the Main Stem of the Chicago River. The Lake Street Bridge is the older of the two with a 1916 construction date. Its lower deck carries vehicles and pedestrians and its upper deck carries CTA "L" trains. The Lake Street Bridge holds the distinction of being the first double-deck bascule bridge constructed in Chicago, replacing a double-deck swing bridge on the same alignment. In order to minimize the disruption of traffic on the existing bridge, the Ketler-Elliott Erection Company of Chicago erected the new bridge in the raised position with the old bridge remaining open to traffic until the new bridge was nearly completed. Trains passed through openings in the raised leaves as they crossed the swing bridge. This method was uncommon for highway bridges, but was typical for railroads, since profit-oriented railroad companies placed a higher importance on maintaining traffic flow during construction. The design of the Lake Street Bridge involved an unusual amount of discussion and argument, and at one point, the city created a commission to study a design for the crossing. The commission recommended a vertical lift bridge for this location, an idea later rejected in favor of the design seen today, which was believed to be more aesthetically pleasing.

Completed in 1984, the modern Randolph Street Bridge resembles a railing-height truss, although the

The construction of the bascule bridge at Lake Street as photographed from the upper deck of the former swing bridge. Note the gap in the deck of the bascule bridge that enabled trains to continue to use the swing bridge during construction.

The opening of the mighty leaves of the Lake Street Bridge is an impressive sight.

Although no longer used in typical operation, some bridges have bells that bridge tenders could ring. The Lake Street Bridge's bell, cast by the Meneeley Bell Company of Troy, New York, is especially beautiful.

bridge is primarily a box girder. The bridge replaced a double-leaf Scherzer rolling lift bascule bridge.

Built in 1913, the Washington Boulevard Bridge is among the first pony truss bascule bridges built in Chicago, a sharp contrast to the modern Randolph Street Bridge immediately north. This bridge was one of the bridges that prompted engineer Joseph Strauss to sue the city over patent infringement because the supports of the bridge's trunnions resembled a similar system patented by Strauss.

The Washington Boulevard Bridge's bridge tender houses stand out with their colorful design, despite being comparatively small.

The slender profile of the Madison Street Bridge contrasts with the massive Civic Opera House in the background.

Constructed in 1922 and located next to the Civic Opera House, the Madison Street Bridge honors the thirty-fifth season of the Lyric Opera of Chicago with its official name, the Lyric Opera Bridge. With its handsomely decorated bridge tender houses and railings, this beautiful bridge is the oldest example of Chicago's unique railing-height truss design. The bridge spans 221 feet between trunnions and has an overall deck width of 72 feet.

The Monroe Street Bridge dates to 1919. The western bascule leaf of this bridge has a special heavier counterweight that allowed the counterweight system for this leaf to take up less space. This was necessary

A previous span at Madison Street was a through truss swing bridge.

37

The raised western leaf of the Monroe Street Bridge dwarfs the attractive bridge tender house.

Visitors arriving at Union Station and exiting on the eastern side of the station complex encounter this view of the Adams Street Bridge.

because the railroad tracks for Union Station ran along the western bank of the river below the road level and there was not enough room for a conventional counterweight system.

Similar to the Monroe Street Bridge, the 1927 Adams Street Bridge has a special layout of the counterweight and machinery for the western bridge leaf due to space limitations caused by the proximity of Union Station. This

deck truss bascule has two bridge tender houses, each displaying the Beaux-Arts design that is a trademark of many of Chicago's bascule bridges.

The Jackson Boulevard Bridge was built in 1915 and opened January 29, 1916, making it the oldest surviving deck truss bascule bridge in Chicago. The bridge has a span of 202 feet between trunnions. The plaque on the bridge mentions that the Sanitary District of Chicago (actually a state agency,

The Jackson Boulevard Bridge has a more smoothly curved bottom chord than the Adams Street Bridge, also a deck truss bascule.

Two sailboats pass under the raised Van Buren Street Bridge as they motor south down the river.

With its Warren truss design, the Congress Parkway Bridge is unique among Chicago's deck truss bascule bridges.

The Chicago Department of Transportation has a group of workers who move from bridge to bridge to raise them for boats during seasonal bridge lifts. Here, workers have raised the Harrison Street Bridge.

today the Metropolitan Water Reclamation District of Greater Chicago), erected the bridge rather than the City of Chicago. While the Sanitary District erected a number of bridges on the Chicago Sanitary and Ship Canal, it was unusual that the agency erected bridges in the downtown area. At that time, the city was investing so heavily in replacing old swing bridges with bascule bridges that the Sanitary District helped out by building the Jackson Boulevard Bridge. The Strauss Bascule Bridge Company designed this aesthetically pleasing bridge. It differs from many of the bascule bridges built by the city because it has a smoothly curved bottom chord rather than one that is composed of straight beams arranged at angles to create the illusion of a curve.

With its attractive trusses and Beaux-Arts bridge tender houses, this was the first movable bridge that truly embodied the aesthetic ideals of the *Plan of Chicago*.

The Van Buren Street Bridge, a railing-height truss bascule, was constructed in 1956. The bridge replaced an 1895 bridge, one of the first Scherzer rolling lift bascule bridges.

Unique among deck truss bascule bridges in Chicago, the Congress Parkway Bridge has diagonal members arranged in a repeating "V"

Buildings and land use around the Roosevelt Road Bridge have changed dramatically over the years, but the bridge itself retains its classic charm.

pattern known as a Warren truss configuration. The bridge has a trunnion-to-trunnion span of 221.5 feet.

The Harrison Street Bridge, a railing-height truss bascule bridge built in 1960, is similar to the Van Buren Street Bridge located two bridges north. The Harrison Street Bridge replaced a deck truss Scherzer rolling lift bascule bridge.

The Roosevelt Road Bridge is a deck truss bascule built in 1928. A viaduct system provides an approach to the bridge. While the bascule leaves that provide a trunnion-to-trunnion span of 204 feet are impressive, the pair of unique cylindrical bridge tender houses is what truly draws the eye. These iconic works of art are unlike any other bridge tender houses in the city.

The Baltimore and Ohio Railroad Chicago Terminal Railroad Bridge stands abandoned in the raised position. Beside it to the south is the St. Charles Air Line Bridge. These railroad bridges are both single-leaf heel-trunnion bascule bridges designed by the Strauss Bascule Bridge Company. Constructed in 1930, the Chicago Terminal Bridge represents the maturation of Joseph Strauss's heel-trunnion design. In contrast, the

These drawings of the St. Charles Air Line Bridge with its original length illustrate how the heel-trunnion bascule system operates.

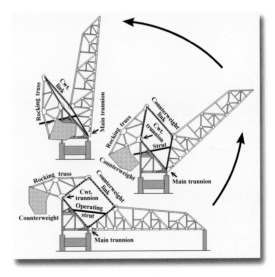

41

This photo shows the Pennsylvania Railroad Bridge Number 458 under construction with unique false work supporting the nearly constructed lift span. Also visible is the swing bridge it replaced.

St. Charles Air Line Bridge has a far more unusual story to tell. It was built in 1919, originally in a slightly different location. In 1919, the South Branch of the Chicago River had not yet been realigned to its current channel. Constructed over the former river alignment, the bridge had the longest bascule leaf in the world, with a 260-foot length. When the river realignment occurred, contractors carefully dismantled and reassembled the St. Charles Air Line Bridge over the new alignment. The new location did not require such a long span, and contractors shortened the truss by 40 feet, making the bridge 220 feet in length.

The trunnion of the single-leaf bascule Eighteenth Street Bridge is located at the left end.

Built in 1967, the Eighteenth Street Bridge was the last bascule bridge built in Chicago using rivets, the traditional fastener for metal bridge construction since the 1800s. Later bridges employed only bolts and welding. With a span from the trunnion of 182 feet, this bridge stands out as one of only two examples of a single-leaf bascule bridge for highway use in Chicago. The bridge is part of a viaduct that carries the road over a city street and railroad tracks.

Pennsylvania Railroad's Bridge Number 458 casts a reflection on calm waters in the early morning.

Bridges with longer spans require larger trusses. For this reason, the trusses of the Canal Street Bridge are very tall.

Large historic industrial buildings surround the Cermak Road Bridge. Together, bridge and buildings make this location a virtual trip back in time.

Bridge Number 458, originally of the Pennsylvania Railroad, is the only vertical lift bridge on the Chicago River. The bridge's pair of towers, measuring 195 feet in height, can raise the 272.8-foot truss to provide as much as 130 feet of clearance for marine traffic. This truss span was the heaviest of any vertical lift in the United States when completed in 1914. During construction, builders employed an unusual falsework that rested on the piers and spread out in a fan-like shape to support the truss span during

The Halsted Street Bridge has two attractive bridge tender houses. The southeast house is clearly visible in this view facing north.

its erection in the raised position. The fan-shaped design kept the falsework out of the water where it would obstruct marine traffic, while providing for the erection of the truss span in the raised position. This allowed the old swing bridge to continue to carry railroad traffic during construction. Designed by the firm of Waddell and Harrington, the bridge remains functional today, carrying a variety of railroad traffic including Metra and Amtrak passenger trains as well as freight.

Constructed in 1949, the Canal Street Bridge is a later example of Chicago's pony truss bascule design. With a span of 254 feet between trunnions, it is the longest pony truss bascule span in Chicago.

The Cermak Road Bridge is the only surviving Scherzer rolling lift highway bascule bridge in Chicago. Although Chicago constructed many Scherzer rolling lift bascule bridges, the city has since demolished all the other examples of this type. Constructed in 1906, the Cermak Road Bridge also stands out nationally as a surviving early example of Scherzer rolling lift technology. The bridge has a trunnion-to-trunnion span of 216 feet.

The 1934 Halsted Street Bridge is a pony truss bascule noted for having three truss lines, which provide a four-lane roadway. The two bridge tender houses display depictions of both the current bridge and the previous bridge at this location, an 1894 vertical lift bridge designed by John Alexander Low Waddell. That bridge was a very early example of its type in the United States.

Constructed in 1974, the Loomis Street Bridge is one of only three highway bascule

The depiction of a ship passing under the former vertical lift bridge at Halsted Street is on the current bascule bridge's tender house.

45

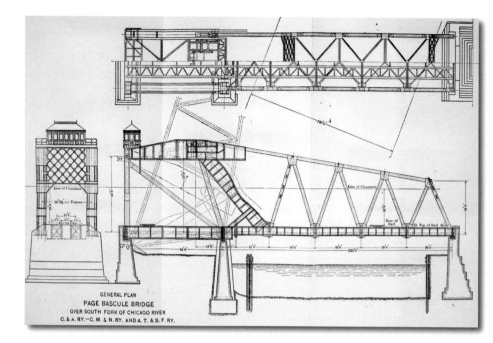

GENERAL PLAN
PAGE BASCULE BRIDGE
OVER SOUTH FORK OF CHICAGO RIVER
C. & A. RY.—C. M. & N. RY. AND A. T. & S. F. RY.

This dimensioned drawing of the Chicago and Alton Railroad Bridge illustrates its Page bascule design.

bridges built in Chicago after 1970. The bridge continues the railing-height truss design the city had used for decades, but typical of modern bridges it is fastened with bolts instead of rivets.

Bridges on the South Branch of the Chicago River open at prescheduled times in the spring and autumn, mainly to let recreational sailboats in and out of Lake Michigan.

The South Fork of the South Branch of the Chicago River is home to the Chicago and Alton Railroad Bridge, the only example of a Page-type bascule bridge in Chicago and one of the few surviving examples of this type in the United States. Many engineers have developed and patented their own ideas for the best bascule bridge design. Most of these designs never gained much ground in terms of actual bridge construction. The Page bascule, a variation of a trunnion bascule bridge, was created and patented by John W. Page and is one such design that was never built in significant numbers. The Chicago and Alton Railroad Bridge was the first Page bascule built for railroad use. The bridge's distinctive visual features include the two 70-ton rack guides with their unusual curved shape and the overhead counterweights which line up with the profile of the through truss, enhancing the aesthetic qualities of the bridge. The bridge has a span from the trunnion of 150 feet. William Mackenzie Hughes of Chicago designed the bridge under Page and Shnable patent. This bridge no longer raises.

CHICAGO SANITARY AND SHIP CANAL TOUR

THE CHICAGO SANITARY AND SHIP CANAL, originally known as the Chicago Drainage Canal, extends southwest from the South Branch of the Chicago River. The canal is 28 miles long and was completed in 1900 to carry Chicago's sewage away from Lake Michigan. It also functioned as a replacement for the older and smaller Illinois and Michigan Canal, allowing boats in the Great Lakes to access the Mississippi River.

This tour works westward from the eastern end of the canal, starting at the Ashland Avenue Bridge. Constructed in 1938, this bridge is a pony truss bascule with three truss lines. This bridge still operates for boats in the spring and autumn. All other movable Chicago Sanitary and Ship Canal bridges between this bridge and the Calumet Sag Channel are no longer operated for boats.

This photo, taken facing north toward the Ashland Avenue Bridge, shows the three truss lines of the bridge.

Previous pages: The Eight Track Railroad Bridge has overhead counterweights that line up with the shape of the truss superstructures. One span of the original fixed deck truss is visible to the right.

The Western Avenue Bridge was built in 1940 as a fixed through plate girder bridge. However, the 21 feet of clearance it provided was not enough for World War II naval vessels to pass. As a result, in 1942, the city converted the bridge into a vertical lift by adding towers that could lift a center section of the bridge. After the war, these towers remained on the bridge for many decades, but the city eventually removed them, returning the bridge to its original fixed design.

In 1900, the Scherzer Rolling Lift Bridge Company completed the Eight Track Railroad Bridge that consisted of four parallel superstructures sharing common piers and abutments. As originally built, each superstructure carried two tracks and included a fixed deck truss span at each end and a special fixed span in between that looked like a through truss but functioned as an arch bridge. The design of the arch structure provided for future conversion into a double-leaf rolling lift bascule bridge in anticipation of a future requirement for a movable bridge to permit passage of boats. By 1907, plans to make the bridge movable were underway, but engineers determined that the center spans could actually be replaced completely with new single-leaf bascule spans for only a small increase in construction cost and with the added benefits of a simpler and more modern design. As a result, Chicago Bridge and Iron Company replaced the old fixed arch span with the distinctive bascule spans seen today, using an updated design created by the Scherzer Rolling Lift Bridge Company, while reusing the original fixed deck truss spans. The pier on which the counterweight end of the leaves and associated mechanical equipment rests alternates since the original four superstructures were so close to each other that there was not enough room

Creative engineering allowed conversion of the fixed Western Avenue Bridge to a vertical lift bridge. Here, the towers are still in place with the lift span fully opened.

The camera captures a brief moment of calm in an otherwise busy evening commute on the California Avenue Bridge.

for all the machinery to be on the same pier. More recently, the deck truss approach spans of the easternmost structure were replaced with deck girders.

The California Avenue Bridge is a pony truss bascule bridge. It is no longer raised for boats, and the city removed the bridge tender house. Despite this, the bridge trusses visually convey its movable past, while continuing to bear the load of traffic.

Located west of California Avenue is the Collateral Channel, a slip that extends north of the Sanitary and Ship Canal. The only crossing is the Chicago and Illinois Western Railway Bridge. It is the only example in Chicago of a Rall bascule, an unusual and rare variation of trunnion bascule. The trunnion rests on a special roller wheel that carries the leaf backwards away from the channel on a horizontal track simultaneously as the bascule leaf rises. Theodor Rall patented the Rall bascule and the Strobel Steel Construction Company controlled the patent.

The combination roller and trunnion of the Chicago and Illinois Western Railway Bridge is visible above the center concrete pier. The girders to the left of this pier conceal the concrete counterweight between them.

The swing bridge located between the Pulaski Road and Kedzie Avenue bridges is about 385 feet long, one of three swing bridges remaining in Chicago on the Chicago Sanitary and Ship Canal.

The Cicero Avenue Bridge has a slender profile, as viewed from a boat.

Between California Avenue and Cicero Avenue, there are three railroad through truss center pier swing bridges. The first is east of Kedzie Avenue, the second between Pulaski Road and Kedzie Avenue, and the third east of Cicero Avenue. The Sanitary District of Chicago directed the construction of these bridges from 1899 to 1900. All three bridges provide a rare look at a type of movable bridge that was once common in Chicago until the functionally superior bascule bridges replaced them.

The Cicero Avenue Bridge is a pony truss bascule that had two truss lines in 1927. In 1966, the city widened the bridge by adding a third truss line. The bridge no longer operates for boats, and the bridge tender houses have been shrouded in sheet metal. This is the last movable bridge on the canal within city limits.

CALUMET RIVER TOUR

LOCATED AT THE SOUTHERN END of Chicago, the Calumet River extends south from Lake Michigan. The Grand Calumet River and the Little Calumet River are two branches of the river. The Calumet–Saganashkee Channel, commonly called the Cal–Sag Channel, connects the Little Calumet River to the Chicago Sanitary and Ship Canal. The Calumet River is the only waterway in Chicago where movable bridges open as needed twenty-four hours a day, primarily for barges. This tour starts from Lake Michigan and proceeds inland.

The Elgin, Joliet, and Eastern Railway Company's Bridge Number 710 is a modern vertical lift bridge. The American Bridge division of U.S. Steel built the bridge in 1974. With trussed towers and a through truss main span, the bridge demonstrates that the basic superstructure design employed in the earliest vertical lift bridges did not change dramatically over the following decades.

The Ewing Avenue Bridge, sometimes called the Ninety-second Street Bridge, was constructed in 1914, and is the oldest highway bascule bridge on the Calumet River. With its span of 128 feet between trunnions, it is the longest remaining example of the earliest style of pony truss bascule built in Chicago.

Constructed in 1958, the Ninety-fifth Street Bridge is the youngest example of a pony truss bascule bridge in Chicago. In the 1980 film *The Blues Brothers* starring John Belushi and Dan Akroyd, the Bluesmobile jumps across this bridge in the raised position.

Located a short distance south of the Ninety-fifth Street Bridge is a unique trio of vertical lift railroad bridges. There were originally four vertical lift bridges at this location, all of similar construction. As originally designed by Waddell and Harrington, the crossing included two vertical lift bridges for the Pittsburgh, Fort Wayne, and Chicago Railway completed in 1913 and two vertical lift bridges for the Lake Shore and Michigan Southern Railway completed in 1915. There are only slight differences in the design details of the 1913 and 1915 bridges. In 1965, one of the Pittsburgh, Fort Wayne, and

Below:
The Ninety-fifth
Street Bridge has
trusses similar to
earlier pony truss
bascule bridges,
but the abutments
and bridge tender
houses have
a simpler
appearance typical
of later bascule
bridges in Chicago.

Chicago Railway bridges was demolished. Tragically, the contractor dropped the span, killing two workers. In 1968, the two Lake Shore and Michigan Southern Railway bridges were abandoned. Fortunately, these bridges were not demolished and were left in the raised position. The remaining Pittsburgh, Fort Wayne, and Chicago Railway Bridge is the only bridge that still carries trains, both freight and Amtrak passenger trains. Alongside these bridges are the remnants of a Strauss bascule bridge constructed in 1913 for the Baltimore and Ohio Chicago Terminal Railroad. At the time of completion, the bridge's 230-foot leaf broke a record for length. After seven decades on the river, the bridge was damaged beyond repair when a boat collided with it and sheared off the massive leaf.

Although a fixed bridge, the Chicago Skyway Toll Bridge bears mention if for no other reason than that it is impossible to ignore. This fixed high-level cantilever through truss was built in 1958. The long approaches that bring the roadway up to the height needed to carry the main span of 650

Above: The Elgin, Joliet, and Eastern Railway Company's Bridge Number 710 is to the right and the Ewing Avenue Bridge to the left. Both bridges are in the raised position.

Left:
The three Waddell and Harrington vertical lift bridges stand as early monuments to modern vertical lift bridge design.

Right:
The 106th Street Bridge's looming pony trusses are hard to ignore when crossing the bridge.

feet over the river demonstrate how movable bridges greatly reduce the footprint of a bridge that crosses navigable waters.

The 100th Street Bridge, the next bridge further inland, and the 106th Street Bridge are similar, although the 106th Street Bridge has an impressively longer 250-foot span, which is why its pony trusses are noticeably taller. The 100th Street Bridge and the 106th Street Bridge were built in 1927 and 1930, respectively.

The Chicago and Western Indiana Railroad Bridge, a vertical lift bridge, now abandoned in the raised position, is a relatively young bridge, built in 1968.

A few feet away is the Torrence Avenue Bridge. Officially named the Henry Ford II Memorial Bridge and dating to 1938, this is the only operable movable

highway bridge remaining in Chicago that is not a bascule bridge. Thomas Pihlfeldt demonstrated that his engineering experience extended beyond the bascule bridge when he undertook the design of the Torrence Avenue Bridge, which features a main span of 276 feet. Pihlfeldt selected the vertical lift for this location because the Calumet River runs at a significant skew to Torrence

Above:
In this photo of the 100th Street Bridge, the Chicago Skyway Toll Bridge soars over the river in the background.

Left:
The Chicago and Western Indiana Railroad Bridge sits fixed in its raised position behind the Torrence Avenue Bridge in the lowered position.

This view shows the southern end of the railroad bridge crossing the Little Calumet River that is actually a disabled and reused bascule span.

Avenue, and the vertical lift was better suited to address this site.

A short distance southwest of the Torrence Avenue Bridge is the Nickel Plate Road Railroad Bridge, a vertical lift bridge and the final movable bridge on the Calumet River. Unlike the Chicago and Western Indiana Railroad Bridge, this one still carries trains.

Crossing the Little Calumet River west of Indiana Avenue on the edge of Chicago city limits, is the final movable bridge on this waterway system. This railroad bridge is a fixed trunnion bascule bridge that remained in place to support a portion of a wider and much longer fixed bridge that was constructed following the widening of the waterway. The counterweights and other operating equipment of the bascule bridge have been removed, and the leaf is partially hidden within the larger bridge.

The tall towers of the Nickel Plate Road Railroad Bridge complement the large through truss lift span.

HISTORIC MOVABLE BRIDGES

THE U.S. GOVERNMENT defines a historic bridge as one listed in or formally eligible for listing in the National Register of Historic Places, a designation given to about twenty of Chicago's movable highway bridges to recognize their historical and technological significance. In addition, the city has a Chicago Landmark designation that recognizes significant structures in the city. More than a dozen bridges, mostly railroad bridges, have been honored in this way, in recognition of exemplary engineering and aesthetic features.

Regardless of official designation, all movable bridges built before 1970 in Chicago display at least one of several historic metal fabrication and construction details not found in modern bridges. Builders constructed these bridges using rivets to fasten the parts of the bridge together. Rivets fell from favor for use in bridge construction by 1970, with welds and bolts favored after that time. While rivets served a utilitarian purpose in the past, they are today a noteworthy record of historical assembly techniques. Rivets are also aesthetically pleasing in appearance. Unlike bolts, each end of a rivet is a smooth, round head that adds visual appeal.

Chicago movable bridges built before 1970 made extensive use of built-up beams, large beams consisting of smaller parts riveted together. Some riveted built-up beams were fabricated with small bars connecting the larger parts of the beam. These bars were

This unusual perspective is the inside of the top chord of the Halsted Street Bridge over the Chicago Sanitary and Ship Canal. The top chord is a riveted built-up beam with lattice bars.

Located east of Kedzie Avenue over the Chicago Sanitary and Ship Canal, this large railroad swing bridge of 479.4 feet broke records for its length when completed in 1900.

often arranged in a repeating "V" pattern called v-lacing or a repeating "X" pattern called lattice or double-lacing. This lacing is a utilitarian feature and adds a pleasing rhythmic pattern to the bridge. Rivets, built-up beams, and lacing are all features not found on modern bridges, and as a result, their preservation is worthwhile. Chicago has an impressive number of surviving movable bridges that display these historical construction details. It should be noted that in the process of repairing and rehabilitating Chicago's movable bridges over the course of their service lives, rivets have sometimes been replaced with bolts and built-up beams have sometimes been replaced with one-piece beams.

From the significance of their engineering design down to the rivets that hold them together, Chicago's movable bridges are an important part of the transportation heritage of the United States and are worthy of preservation.

PLACES TO VISIT

THE BRIDGES

Chicago is a large, busy, and dense city where a car can sometimes be a burden. Fortunately, many of Chicago's bridges are not difficult to access without a car. Below are a few touring ideas and suggestions with an eye toward avoiding the use of a car. The list of ideas is not exhaustive. Note that with the exception of the Cherry Avenue Bridge, railroad bridges are private property and not open to the public.

NORTH BRANCH CHICAGO RIVER

Bridges as far north as Ohio Street are easy to visit on foot using local streets. Note that the Ohio Street Bridge is not open to pedestrians. The Cherry Avenue Bridge and the former location of the North Avenue bascule bridge are easy to access directly from the CTA Red Line's North/Clybourn train station, which is less than a half mile away. Visiting the remaining bridges on the North Branch of the Chicago River requires a car or some combination of public transportation.

MAIN STEM CHICAGO RIVER

Bridges on the Main Stem of the Chicago River are easy to visit on foot. Wacker Drive, on the south side of the river, provides convenient access to all bridges as far east as Columbus Drive. At the south end of the Columbus Drive Bridge, a stairway down to a riverwalk provides convenient access to Lake Shore Drive. This riverwalk also extends westward from Columbus Drive, running under the bridges as far west as State Street. There are plans to extend the river walk to Lake Street on the South Branch Chicago River. For a boat tour, water taxi boats are a quick and inexpensive way to see the bridges.

The Shoreline Water Taxi (blue boats) route between the Navy Pier Ogden Slip dock and the Union Station dock at 200 S. Wacker Drive on the South Branch Chicago River provides the most complete tour, although the yellow Chicago Water Taxis also travel much of the Main Stem of the Chicago River.

SOUTH BRANCH CHICAGO RIVER

Bridges on the South Branch of the Chicago River as far south as Harrison Street can be easily viewed on foot. Between Randolph Street and Jackson Boulevard, property owners on the west side of the river have made privately owned plazas and sidewalks. Otherwise, nearby public streets can be used to access and view bridges. An exception is that pedestrians are not allowed on the Congress Parkway Bridge. A Chicago Water Taxi (yellow boats) route from the base of Trump Tower, on the north side of the Main Stem of the Chicago River west of Michigan Avenue, runs west and south to Ping Tom Memorial Park, located between the Eighteenth Street Bridge and the Pennsylvania Railroad Bridge Number 458. The park offers the best views of these two bridges. The Ashland train station platform on the CTA Orange Line is the only way to get a close look at the Chicago and Alton Railroad Bridge on foot. Note that the Ashland Avenue Bridge is about a half mile north of the station as well.

SANITARY AND SHIP CANAL

The railroad bridges of the Sanitary and Ship Canal generally can be seen only from a distance when on foot or in a car. While a car or the CTA bus and train system can be used to access the highway bridges, the best way to view the canal bridges is from a boat. While no water taxis or tour boats regularly travel the canal, the Richard J. Daley Boat Launch is available on the south side of the canal just west of the Western Avenue Bridge. A small craft such as a 12-foot fishing boat with a 10-hp outboard is sufficient to visit the bridges on the canal. Yield to and be aware of barge traffic and the waves they create.

CALUMET RIVER

Accessibility to bridges is similar to that of the Sanitary and Ship Canal. While a car or buses can be used to access highway bridges, it is difficult to get close to the railroad bridges. A boat is a good alternative way to see the bridges. Again, a small fishing boat is sufficient, and you should be watchful for barge traffic. A small boat launch is available at Waterfront Pub, located at 14042 Croissant Drive, Burnham, IL 60633. From here, you can work your way northbound, passing through the T. J. O'Brien Lock and Dam along the way.

OTHER PLACES TO VISIT

MCCORMICK BRIDGEHOUSE & CHICAGO RIVER MUSEUM

376 N. Michigan Ave, Chicago, IL 60610
www.bridgehousemuseum.org
This museum is located in the southwestern bridge tender house of the Michigan Avenue (DuSable) Bridge. The museum offers access to a room under the bridge tender house where you can view the trunnion, motors, braking systems, and gears of the Michigan Avenue Bridge. Some of the old electrical and operating equipment from the bridge tender building are on display in the museum as well. The remainder of the museum focuses on the history and conservation of the Chicago River.

FURTHER READING

Holth, Nathan. *HistoricBridges.org*. This website documents thousands of
historic bridges by providing numerous photos, videos, detailed
information, and commentary, including extensive coverage of Chicago.
Many of the Chicago listings also include historical photos and old
publications related to the bridges. Website: www.historicbridges.org

Phillips, James S. *Chicago Loop Bridges*. This website includes information,
photos, and video for eighteen movable bridges within the downtown
Loop. It includes connections to popular culture and current news and
events relating to the bridges. Website: www.chicagoloopbridges.com

Phillips, James S. *Two Miles—Eighteen Bridges: A Walk Along the Chicago River*.
2008. This digital book considers the bridges of Chicago with a focus on
exploring how the city's movable bridges evolved over the decades. It
also includes "fact sheets" and other information for eighteen of the
bridges on the Main and South branches of the Chicago River. The book
is available for viewing and purchase from chicagoloopbridges.com.

*Chicago River Bascule Bridges, Spanning Chicago River & Its North & South
Branches, Chicago, Cook County, IL*. Library of Congress, Prints &
Photographs Division, HAER ILL, 16-CHIG, 137. A production of the
National Park Service's Historic American Engineering Record, this
document includes a detailed technical discussion regarding the
development of movable bridges in Chicago from 1890 to 1910.
Website: www.loc.gov/pictures/item/il0705/

INDEX